Art Deco
House Styles

Art Deco
House Styles

Trevor Yorke

COUNTRYSIDE BOOKS
NEWBURY BERKSHIRE

First published 2011
© Trevor Yorke 2011
Reprinted 2013

COUNTRYSIDE BOOKS
3 Catherine Road
Newbury, Berkshire

To view our complete range of books,
please visit us at
www.countrysidebooks.co.uk

ISBN 978 1 84674 247 7

Designed by Peter Davies, Nautilus Design
Produced through MRM Associates, Reading
Printed by Berforts Information Press, Oxford

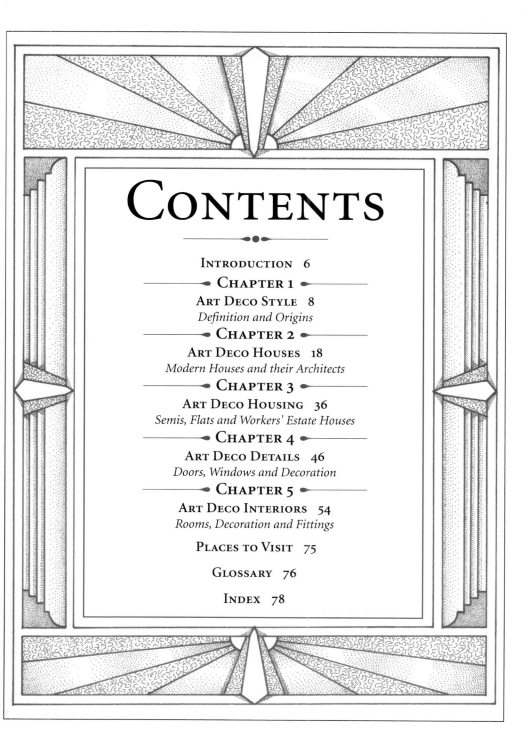

CONTENTS

INTRODUCTION   6

● CHAPTER 1 ●

ART DECO STYLE   8
Definition and Origins

● CHAPTER 2 ●

ART DECO HOUSES   18
Modern Houses and their Architects

● CHAPTER 3 ●

ART DECO HOUSING   36
Semis, Flats and Workers' Estate Houses

● CHAPTER 4 ●

ART DECO DETAILS   46
Doors, Windows and Decoration

● CHAPTER 5 ●

ART DECO INTERIORS   54
Rooms, Decoration and Fittings

PLACES TO VISIT   75

GLOSSARY   76

INDEX   78

INTRODUCTION

— • • —

Most styles of house fall into neat categories: there are the rustic timber-framed structures, symmetrical Classical façades and brick Gothic buildings, with details from each being revived and reworked every few generations. Even today, new housing estates are full of homes that, although accommodating the latest technology, are inspired by these past designs since most owners in this country find comfort and pride in traditional British building styles. Yet there was one moment when in between these reassuring rustic façades could be found something stark, foreign and shocking: white, flat-roofed houses, with curved metal windows and bold geometric patterns – the time was the 1930s and the style is known as Art Deco.

There is far more to Art Deco, though, than these familiar and unique buildings. Art Deco was a reaction against traditional forms and the tumultuous times. It could be luxurious, as represented in Hollywood musicals or adaptations of Agatha Christie's *Poirot* books, exotic as inspired by the tomb of Tutankhamun, or streamlined and modern as shown on trains like the *Mallard* and Saturday morning screenings of *Flash Gordon*. It encompassed all aspects of designs, from huge factories down to the handles on a door, using new materials like chromium and Bakelite and the latest tastes from Europe and America. Think of the Hoover building in West London, the Chrysler skyscraper in New York, and the curving façades of Odeon cinemas and you will start to recognise this dynamic and distinctive style.

This book sets out to explain the background to Art Deco, introduce the most notable architects of the style and illustrate the unique features of Art Deco houses, using clearly-labelled drawings and photographs. The first chapter defines the style, explains how it developed and its effect upon contemporary and later culture. The second chapter describes the finest houses and the work of the leading architects, giving a brief biography of each and examples of their work. The next chapter shows the mass-produced housing that imitated the work of these top designers and the streamlined semis that are the familiar face of Art Deco in this country. The fourth chapter is packed with line drawings and photographs of key features and distinctive details that can help identify the style and provide guidance for those wanting to select authentic pieces when renovating a house. The final part looks inside at the rooms and describes their original appearance and the style of decoration, furniture and fittings that could be found.

For anyone who simply wants to recognise the style, understand the contribution of key characters and appreciate what makes Art Deco houses special, this book will be a colourful and an easy-to-follow introduction to the subject. If the reader is fortunate enough to own such a house, then the illustrations and text will hopefully enlighten them as to its value and aid any planned renovation or redecoration. For those of us who can but look on and admire, I hope the book helps clarify the true essence of the style and why it is such a unique and valuable contribution to a street, a community or even a town; one that is gradually gaining appreciation and is in desperate need of protection for future generations.

Trevor Yorke

www.trevoryorke.co.uk
Follow me on Facebook

FIG 1.1: CARRERAS CIGARETTE FACTORY, CAMDEN, LONDON: *Egyptian-style decoration inspired by Howard Carter's discovery of the tomb of Tutankhamun in 1922 and popularised by Hollywood is distinctive of the earlier phases of Art Deco.*

ART DECO STYLE

Definition and Origins

Art Deco is the style that reflected many of the themes from the inter-war years. The 1920s and 30s, squeezed between the cataclysmic world wars, were shaped by the economic effects and great loss of life of the first conflict and then a growing fear of the second war. This contrasted with a feeling of optimism in the initial belief that people had survived the 'war to end all wars' and could escape from the drudgery within which many still found themselves trapped – moods that were captured in images of jazz, outrageous fashion, Hollywood films and a love of the sun. Many found solace by surrounding themselves with traditional forms, their homes imitating Tudor or Georgian structures. Others, however, looked to the future and revelled in modernity and the exotic, having houses with streamlined, white exteriors and bold, geometric patterns within, inspired by designs from across the globe and using new materials. It is this latter group of buildings and objects that, although known at the time by a variety of terms, are today generally bundled together under the title 'Art Deco'.

Your chances of enjoying the benefits of a new home in this style depended very much on where you lived and the class into which you were born. The working masses,

FIG 1.2: *Art Deco could combine modernity and luxury, giving mass-produced objects a luxurious veneer. It could be glossy and exotic or stark and modern, but as in these clocks dating from the mid 1930s there was an underlining use of geometric shapes and horizontal lines as opposed to the floral and naturalistic shapes of styles before the First World War.*

Model 130.
Jacobean.
3½ in. silvered
dial. Chromium **37/6**
bezel.

Model 136.
Oak, ebonised side
pieces and plinth and **85/-**
chromium straps.

For A.C. Mains, 200/250
volts, 50 cycles, time-
controlled frequency.
Obtainable from high-
class Jewellers, Electrical
and Radio Dealers.

FERRANTI
ELECTRIC CLOCKS

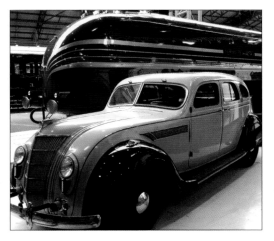

FIG 1.3: *A love affair with machines and a delight in speed inspired the streamlining displayed on this contemporary car and steam engine on view at the National Railway Museum at York. This would also have some influence on the design of houses and goods. This was the period in which sun bathing was first seen as beneficial and fashionable, hence a craving for light, sun-trap windows and sun lounges.*

especially those stuck in terraced slums within old industrial centres, suffered as factories closed in the wake of new global competition; the General Strike of 1926 and the Jarrow March of 1936 are vivid reminders of the struggle faced by millions. Yet, new opportunities in the car, aircraft, electrical appliance and chemical industries, mainly in towns and cities of the south of England and the Midlands, created an expanding number of white collar workers and managers. This was such that those who would be termed 'middle class' nearly doubled in the space of a few decades to account for around a third of the population by 1939. It was this group who would be the principal driving force behind the rapid growth of suburbia in this period.

This wave of new building, which engulfed the countryside around many towns and cities, comprised partly select developments and detached houses built by leading architects and talented local builders (some of the finest Art Deco structures and notable designers are described in Chapter 2), while the rest of the stock was private homes erected by speculative builders or new estates rented by the working classes (those in this style are covered in Chapter 3). Despite the more extreme forms of modern buildings being devoid of ornamentation, most Art Deco houses have characteristic doors, windows and decorative features, which are illustrated in Chapter 4, while inside the home, where the style was more readily accepted, the appearance of the rooms and types of fixtures and fittings found there are described in Chapter 5.

ORIGINS

The Three Arts

It is typical that you get no 'Arts' in over a thousand years of design and then suddenly three come along all at once! Arts and Crafts, Art Nouveau and Art Deco were all terms used to describe some of the leading designs in the period from the late 1800s up until the outbreak of the Second World War and although these titles can often be confusing they had distinctive characteristics and sources of inspiration, which clearly differentiate them. At the same time, they shared many of the same principles and objectives. Before looking at a more precise definition of what we regard as Art Deco, it is worth briefly describing these other styles and influences in design, which laid the foundations for this explosion of the exotic and modern, principally in the ten years from 1925.

The Arts and Crafts movement was ignited by the writings of John Ruskin and the dynamic character of William Morris, with architects and designers working individually or within guilds, producing buildings that were inspired by old farms and manor houses but in new forms using locally-sourced materials. In the late 19th century the design of decorative goods was generally poor and one of the key aims of Arts and Crafts practitioners was to raise the status of craftsmanship to that of the Fine Arts and improve the standard of British goods. Their methods of doing so looked back to a mystical medieval past and a rejection of machine and mass-produced goods. This meant, though, that their products became expensive and rather elitist, failing to liberate the suppressed factory worker as this mainly Socialist-inspired movement had intended. Despite this, the establishment of design schools, their honesty with structures and materials (not trying to disguise a building as something it was not), their new approach to interior design, and their responsibility for all elements from the structure of the building down to the smallest detail of the interior would inspire the following generation in Britain, on the Continent and in America.

At the same time in Europe, the most distinctive form of decorative design was Art Nouveau (named after La Maison de l'Art Nouveau, Siegfried Bing's art gallery, which opened in Paris in 1895). Here, nature was the key theme, with objects featuring twisting plant stems and exotic flowers, which become part of the structure. The distinctive lettering of the Paris Metro and Tiffany lamps are two of the most familiar examples

FIG 1.4: *An Art Nouveau-style Tiffany lamp (left) in which the fitting appears to be organically growing out of the base and inspired by nature, as were many Arts and Crafts objects, and a later Art Deco radio (right) with strong geometric shapes radiating from the sun-like dial. The Arts and Crafts icon William Morris was one of the first to believe that art should be designed to meet the ideals of society and that there should be no distinction between form and function.*

of this unique but short-lived style, one that only made an impact in the British home in decorative pieces inside and some of the coloured-glass patterns in windows. By the nature of its sinuous forms, Art Nouveau did not lend itself to mass production and many of those who went on to form new groups and associations in the opening decades of the 20th century did so partly as a rejection of this style and traditional teachings but also in an attempt to reconcile the gap between art and industry. It would be this new generation of architects and designers who would be the leading lights of Art Deco.

Developments in Europe and America

Unlike Arts and Crafts and Art Nouveau, the inspiration for Art Deco came from across the globe. Charles Rennie Mackintosh was one of the few in this country to use geometric forms in his work. Although not widely appreciated here at the time, he was of greater influence on the Continent especially with regard to the Vienna Secession, which was formed in Austria 1897 as a reaction against the conservative local academy and its promotion of work based upon historic styles (secession is the act of withdrawing from an organisation). The Wiener Werkstatte (Viennese workshops) co-founded in 1903 by Josef Hoffmann, one of the designers who would leave the Vienna Secession over artistic differences, promoted the idea of designing every detail of a project and introduced a new abstract and geometric

DESIGNED BY ALVAR AALTO FOR

Finmar

FURNITURE OF THE FUTURE FOR THE HOME OF TO-DAY

FIG 1.5: *It was not until the 1930s that designers started to understand the properties of industrial materials and began making products that could be both attractive and yet be mass-produced, achieving the ambitions of earlier movements through the acceptance of the machine and modern technology. These plywood pieces by the famous Finnish architect Alvar Aalto were still too hard and uncompromising for most tastes; Modernist designs lacked the cosiness that was preferred by the public and were viewed as rather elitist and chic.*

style of buildings and goods. The principles and works of the Arts and Crafts movement had been studied by the German Hermann Muthesius, who back in his native country helped establish a state-sponsored organisation, the Deutsche Werkbund (German Work Federation), in 1907. Unlike their English forebears, this group intended to make closer links between art and industry, designing objects with functional simplicity so as to be suitable for mass production, principally to make German goods more competitive on the world market. It included Walter Gropius and Ludwig Mies van der Rohe in its ranks, two of the pioneers of modern architecture. At the same time, in France, a new style of art in which the painter disassembled objects and then rearranged them in an abstract form, looked at from a number of viewpoints, was being developed in part by Pablo Picasso. Cubism, as it became known, had influence on later architects due to this new approach to design and its intersecting planes and geometric, stepped and angled forms.

After the First World War, two distinct styles developed, both of which sought closer bonds between art and industry and form and function, and a belief in the concept of total art. One was inspired by primitive American and African art and, after the 1922 discovery of Tutankhamun's tomb, by Ancient Egyptian pieces, resulting in highly luxurious and exotic decorative work; the other was a continuation of the development of a more functional and accessible, modern style. Both were displayed at the influential Exposition Internationale des Arts Décoratifs et Industriels Modernes held in Paris in 1925 (it was around the time of the exhibition's revival in 1966 that the phrase Art Deco was first coined). This was designed to help increase French exports of the decorative arts and integrate their design further with machine production. Despite the ideals, much of what was displayed reflected the new, exotic style that had developed in France since before the war. It included distinctive luxurious furniture featuring

FIG 1.6: THE CHRYSLER BUILDING, NEW YORK, USA: *One of the most iconic Art Deco buildings, it was designed by William Van Alen and completed in 1930 with its distinctive stainless steel sunbursts in the upper floors. The stepped tops of skyscrapers was due to zoning laws from 1916, which forbade them to be a solid mass.*

beautiful marquetry and decorative fittings created by skilled craftsmen, which was clearly unsuitable for mass production. After the Exposition these exotic pieces still filled niche markets but it was the more functional and simplified modern work that became, by the 1930s, the dominant style for furniture, interior decoration and appliances; one suitable for industrial production so that it would fulfil the Modernists' ideal of having good design available to all.

FIG 1.7: GROPIUS HOUSE, LINCOLN, MASS, USA: *Walter Gropius, the former head of the Bauhaus, like many of his compatriots fled Nazi Germany in the 1930s. He moved first to Britain and then to America where he designed this Modernist house for himself in 1938, featuring furniture from his colleague Marcel Breuer. Modernism was less a distinct group of designers and more a trend away from traditional forms of building. Its leading light was Le Corbusier, the Swiss-born architect who was key in making what at the time was termed the International Style popular in Europe and America and for referring to the house as 'a machine for living in'. His rejection of decoration and elitism was rather at odds, though, with the luxurious strand of Art Deco that had developed in France during the 1920s.*

The modern style in the post-war period blossomed in groups like the Dutch De Stijl who explored geometric and abstract forms with use of strong colours, and Russian Constructivism, which celebrated the machine as an integral part of its art. One of the most influential groups in creating this new modern style was the Bauhaus (meaning 'School of Building'), founded in Germany 1919 by Walter Gropius. They produced wallpaper, light fittings, furniture and textiles that were suitable for mass production. Although they produced little in the way of housing, Gropius did appreciate the new direction in which building design was going, stating that 'we want an architecture adapted to our world of machines, radios and fast cars'. The Nazis, however, despised the school and what it saw as foreign influence and it was closed under political pressure in 1933, with many of the artists fleeing to Britain and the United States. America had declined to display work at the 1925 Paris Exposition as it did not feel it had art of sufficient originality to meet their criteria. Instead it sent experts to study the exhibits and bring back ideas to boost its own design industry. Here a new style developed, epitomised by New York skyscrapers and the sets on Hollywood musicals. It was termed 'Jazz Moderne' and lay somewhere between the exotic and modern. Buildings inspired by the machine, speed and the obsession of industry with streamlining became more dominant in the 1930s. This, in turn, began to change under the influence of the immigrant Modernist designers from Europe later in the decade.

British Art Deco

Despite having been at the forefront of technology in the 19th century, Britain had, at the same time, developed an insular and rather backwards approach to the design of houses. We were suspicious of foreign styles, instead using our own historic buildings for inspiration and only really creating something inventive in the hands of the finest Arts and Crafts architects. New items in the house, such as bathrooms and radios, were fitted in wooden boxes to make them appear more traditional. This ingrained attitude continued to a large extent in the 1920s and 30s with the more extreme Modernist houses and products viewed as elitist and left wing and only certain aspects of European and American Art Deco finding favour in the average home. Although some details of the exterior and interior fittings were readily accepted, the overall stark appearance clashed with our love of cosiness and decoration; and the sun lounging flat roofs were at odds with our inclement weather!

The Paris Exposition of 1925 was therefore viewed with suspicion by many. Only a few of our leading designers took

FIG 1.8: *The most common Art Deco form of building was cinemas, luxurious and modern structures often referred to as 'Odeon-style', as with this extraordinary example from Rayners Lane, London (originally designed to represent an elephant).*

part, with people like Ambrose Heal (of Heal's, London) and Gordon Russell exhibiting their furniture. There had been some steps along the lines of European attempts to integrate art and mass production: the British Design and Industries Association, founded in 1915, had echoed others in stating that sound design was firstly about fitness for use, and its own publications helped to promote modern architecture in the early 1930s. Wells Coates and Partners was established in 1929, two years later being re-branded Isokon (from Isometric Unit Construction). It produced modern pieces of furniture and most notably the Lawn Road Flats in North London, which are often referred to as the Isokon Building (see Chapter 2). Walter Gropius designed furniture for them after he arrived from Germany in 1934, living in one of the apartments at Lawn Road until he left for the United States three years later; with one of his colleagues at the Bauhaus, Marcel Breuer, taking over his role.

The modern strain of Art Deco, branded here at the time as Ultra Modern or the International Style (after an exhibition of the same name at the Museum of Modern Art in New York in 1932), had made little impact by the mid 1930s. An example is the Daily Mail Ideal Home Exhibition of 1934, which contained the 'Village of Tomorrow'. This featured white, flat-roofed houses by leading designers who emphasised the advantages of this type of structure: it gave the owner an extra room (on top of the roof), the ability to easily add another storey if required, and to make maximum use of available sunlight (see Fig 2.3). However, at the exhibition in the following year they had all but gone: pitched roofs were preferred by the public. A style that found greater favour, especially with the younger generation, was a watered-down version of the International Style mixed with aspects of American streamlined buildings, referred to as Moderne (sometimes called Streamline Moderne or Sun-trap houses). It was usually a form of surface decoration applied to standard semis, with white rendered walls, characteristic curved glass ends to bay windows and a few geometric decorative patterns.

It was the Modernist house that was to have a more lasting influence though; the Streamline Moderne is just a distinctive feature of the 1930s. After the Second World War the crippled economy, shortages of materials and a desire amongst some for a bright new future opened the way for a more general acceptance of Modernism, at least a type softened by a facing of traditional hanging tiles and weatherboarding. As the chronic housing shortage, which was to last through into the 1960s, forced the authorities to build as many homes as they could in a short space of time, open-plan designs meant houses and flats could be made smaller without the occupants feeling cramped.

FIG 1.9: THE DE LA WARR PAVILION, BEXHILL-ON-SEA, SUSSEX: *It was in seaside resorts that the plain, white streamlined curves of Art Deco seemed more acceptable, as with this famous Modernist pavilion designed by Erich Mendelsohn in collaboration with Serge Chermayeff in 1934.*

However, our obsession with cosy, traditional, village-style houses since the 1980s means that inter-war Modernist homes are still shocking today. New Eco houses, which invariably are modern in style, are marvelled at on television but few new estates are built in this form, while the mortgage provider and private buyer have reservations about the durability of new materials and the dreaded flat roof. Ironically, some elements of the Moderne and traditional styles, which so characterised the 1930s' semi, are finding their way back onto new houses, these having reached such an age as now to be an acceptable and reassuring part of our culture.

FIG 1.10: *Art Deco is most notably displayed on commercial buildings, cinemas and shops where its modern form suited certain companies' profiles. Early examples have stepped profiles to the top of the building, white exteriors usually made up of glazed tiles (top examples), monumental doorways (centre right) and stylised Egyptian or Classical details. By the 1930s, exteriors are less decorative and had streamlined curves and angled steel windows. The most notable example, however, is the Hoover Building along the A40 in West London, which displays all the finest Jazz and Streamline Moderne features (bottom left and right).*

CHAPTER 2

FIG 2.1: *Luxurious housing estates and desirable streets lined with Mock Tudor and Neo Georgian houses suddenly woke up one morning to find stark white modern houses such as this example on their doorstep, a scattering of modernity still as shocking today as it was in the 1930s.*

ART DECO HOUSES

Modern Houses and their Architects

Styles

For those with the money to employ an architect or in the market to buy a house designed by one, there was a wide choice of styles from which to choose. In the 1920s, Neo Georgian with symmetrical fronted brick houses, usually featuring hipped roofs, short casement windows with leaded glass and prominent rainwater traps and down-pipes on each side of the façade (actually inspired by houses built in the decades before the Georgian period), and Mock Tudor with distinctive dark brickwork, timber-framing (usually cladding) and an asymmetrical front or eclectic mixes of rustic features inspired by the Arts and Crafts movement were the preferred choices. On the grandest houses a playful and colourful Classical style inspired by the work of architects like Sir Edwin Lutyens shortly before the First World War was popular. Despite the traditional exterior, however, the inside of these houses could have luxurious and modern fixtures and fittings, which we would term Art Deco in style.

By the early 1930s, these more traditional houses were joined by the latest trends from Europe and America – the International and Moderne styles – often slightly

FIG 2.2: ELTHAM PALACE, LONDON: *This rather eclectic and lively façade full of traditional and Classical features hides one of the most modern interiors of the 1930s. The building was completed in 1936 for Stephen and Virginia Courtauld, with stunning and luxurious rooms and the latest electrical fittings. It now belongs to English Heritage and is currently the only Art Deco house open to the public.*

Flat roofs.

Sun lounge.

Sun roof.

Geometric patterned railings.

Concrete roof overhangs.

Metal framed windows with horizontal bars.

Plain white or brick walls.

Horizontal features.

Built in garage with hinged wooden doors.

Front doors with simple geometric glazing.

FIG 2.3: *An International Style house with labels of its distinctive features. This British version of Modernism (also referred to as the Horizontal Style or Ultra Modern) was named after an exhibition titled 'The International Style' held at the Museum of Modern Art, New York in 1932.*

watered down to suit our more conservative tastes. They are characterised by their use of modern ideas and materials: white walls, steel-framed windows, glass bricks and the option of having a flat roof intended for use as a sun lounging area. The domestic face of Modernism was branded the International Style, with the function of each room taking control of the exterior arrangement, and a strong horizontal emphasis occasionally intersected by a vertical feature. Surfaces were devoid of decoration so the eye could appreciate their dramatic, sharp-edged form, with distinctive long rows of dark windows and the occasional grouping formed into a pattern breaking up the plain walls.

The Moderne (or Streamline Moderne) was a more popular style, using details from Modernist buildings and streamlined structures from America. Most were characterised by the use of curved glass sun-trap windows, horizontal bands across the walls, and the use of the sun-ray, chevron or bold geometric pattern in the glass. Some, however, were inspired by houses from the west coast of America and seen on films. This Hollywood Moderne style was more exotic, often with a conventional structure and tall, hipped roof but covered in distinctive bright green, or occasionally blue, tiles with white walls below, decorative metal railings across balconies and often a palm or similar tree in the garden to complete the picture.

It was also common for builders to make houses with an eclectic mix of features so although it is these Moderne styles that we now term Art Deco, elements of the

FIG 2.4: *Hollywood Moderne style houses were inspired by homes from the west coast of America with distinctive green glazed roof tiles often on top of a conventional symmetrical planned structure and the odd palm tree to complete the effect.*

FIG 2.5: *A Streamline Moderne house, with labels of its distinctive features. Although, as in this example, the façade was generally plain, three or more horizontal bands (between the upper windows) or raised geometric designs were often added.*

International Style could be incorporated. Today, the term 'Modernism' has limited appeal to the public and many of these purely functional houses are confusingly being branded Art Deco by estate agents and owners because of its greater appeal!

Materials

Art Deco structures were characterised by the use of modern materials or at least ones that were new to this form of housing. Concrete had been invented by the Romans and was reintroduced in the second half of the 19th century but was only considered for exposed walling here in the inter-war years. Poured in between wooden shutters with metal reinforcement rods or mesh, concrete made durable and quick to erect walls and floors

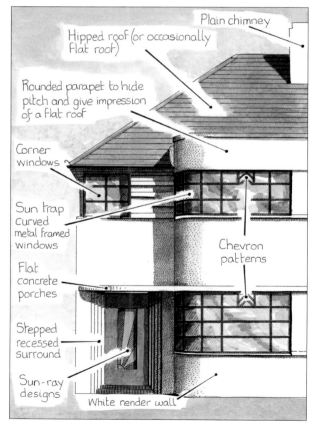

Plain chimney

Hipped roof (or occasionally Flat roof)

Rounded parapet to hide pitch and give impression of a Flat roof

Corner windows

Sun trap Curved metal framed windows

Flat concrete porches

Chevron patterns

Stepped recessed surround

Sun-ray designs

White render wall

(this form of house was not necessarily any cheaper than a brick structure at this date). In many cases, however, concrete was only used for part of the structure, such as the foundations, floors and sometimes pre-cast features like curved porches. It was a step too far for many owners and builders who were not confident with this new material, so conventional brick structures were rendered over and painted white to appear modern!

The International and many of the Moderne-styled houses were designed by the architect or builder to incorporate a flat roof although this was optional. Despite the appeal of a large area on top of the house for sun bathing, the idea of being on public

FIG 2.6: *Bricks with a wavy pattern pressed into their surface were a distinctive feature of 1930s' houses that remained popular into the 1950s.*

show to one's neighbours clashed with our generally reserved and private nature. Also, the realism over our climate and problems with rain penetrating through a flat surface meant the majority of houses were built with a pitched roof. These would usually be covered in small clay tiles or larger Roman tiles but bright green glazed pantiles (often imported from Spain) were popular on more exclusive Moderne houses.

Steel was another new material available, being used for window frames, railings and vertical poles to hold up overhanging roofs and porches (see Chapter 4). A distinctive feature of Art Deco houses was the use of glass in a wide variety of forms and finishes. From the 1890s through to the 1920s, it had only been used as plain sheets or pieces in windows with coloured floral or heraldic patterns in the tops of traditional style houses. By the 1930s, however, simple geometric patterns replaced these styles and the glass fitted could have a textured finish rather than colour to define the design. Glass bricks

CRITTALL WINDOWS

Will always work properly.
Last far longer than wood.
Are thoroughly weather-tight.
Do not swell, warp or shrink.
Can be cleaned from inside.
Have forged bronze fittings.

THE CRITTALL

MANUFACTURING CO LTD

HEAD OFFICE ✦ 210 HIGH HOLBORN ✦ WC1

FIG 2.7: *Crittall were the manufacturers of the metal-framed windows that are so distinctive of Art Deco houses (see also Silver End in Chapter 3 and examples in Chapter 4)*

by companies such as Lenscrete were also used in the 1930s for the first time in the domestic housing market.

Despite these experiments with new materials, the vast majority of houses built in the inter-war years were made from traditional brick and timber. These structures had evolved from their Edwardian counterparts, with cavity walls now widespread and steel ties holding an inner and outer face of brick together; and the space between providing an air gap to aid insulation and reduce damp penetration. Foundations were improved upon, with concrete used to provide a firm base for the brick walls, which were stepped out upon it to spread the load better. Reducing rising

FIG 2.8: *Glass bricks were introduced into the most modern houses.*

damp in a house had always been problematic and the favoured method in this period was to use a line of bitumen within the walls, just above the ground floor. Slate set in cement or a couple of courses of Staffordshire blue bricks were older solutions that were also used. Before the First World War the timber ground floor was raised above the soil and air bricks vented the space to reduce the problem. Although this method was still used in the 1920s and 30s it became common for concrete to form a solid ground floor, sometimes with timber boards set in bitumen across the top. Although much of the internal structure was formed using timber, a new product, breeze or cinder block (made from waste from gasworks or similar and compressed into a building block), was increasingly used for internal walls. The vertical sides of door frames extending up to the ceiling is a sign where they were used (this was done to strengthen the wall, which otherwise was not keyed into the wooden joists).

FIG 2.9: *Green pantiles (left) and Roman tiles (right) are distinctive of inter-war housing, although smaller clay tiles were still the most common form of roofing tile.*

Plans

The International style with its stark white walls was not just a visual shock but heralded a different approach to planning. By using concrete, which could rest upon columns or be cantilevered out, the interior could be freed from the need to have load-bearing walls. Hence, long lines of windows, glass bricks and movable partitions made rooms light and flexible. The use of a flat roof also gave the architect further freedom as it could cover any shape or form of plan whereas a pitched roof put certain restrictions in place in order to support its greater load and because of the limitations on dimensions due to the pitch at which it had to be set. Despite the advantages of these concrete structures and open interiors advertised by designers, especially in the early 1930s, the plan of most houses was still largely conventional, with social changes rather than architects' opinions affecting the arrangement of rooms.

Houses built in the suburbs where land was cheap could

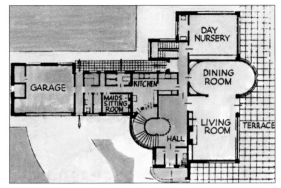

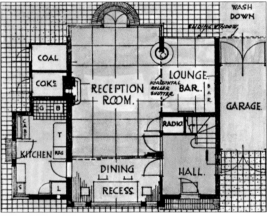

FIG 2.10: *Two plans of modern houses from the mid 1930s, with elements of open planning between reception rooms and a garage built into the structure.*

spread out over their plot and give the architect greater freedom. The International Style house could range from a plain horizontal block to a series of intersecting units, although some of the more exceptional examples featured wings at different angles. Houses built in a Y-shape with two wide arms welcoming visitors had first been devised by Arts and Crafts architects and were widely used on large houses, mainly in the 1920s. The greater size of the suburban plot also meant the wider side of the house could face the road, thus making the house appear larger and more imposing than earlier terraces and semis where the short end was seen by the public. Architects of Moderne and International Style houses also liked to maximise sunlight so made a big point of using large expanses of glass and ensured that the principal rooms for relaxing were facing south.

The most notable change to the house was caused because servants who had been plentiful in the late 19th century were now so hard to find. This shortage meant that most houses were now designed with only a daily maid or cook in mind and no space allowed for live-in staff. As a result, the service rooms had to be more presentable and easier to manage than those in late Victorian houses. Now the lady of the house was expected to become more involved with cooking and cleaning. The old rear extensions with scullery and storage were gone, and the kitchen in larger houses, usually still with a

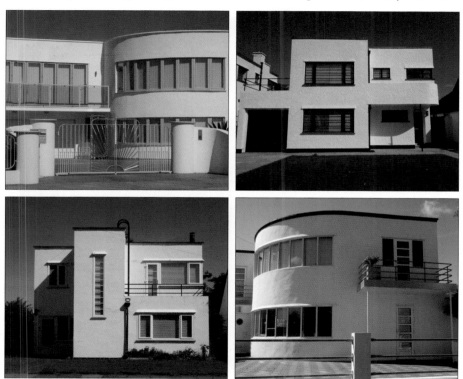

FIG 2.11: FRINTON PARK ESTATE, FRINTON, ESSEX: *In 1934 the South Coast Development Company purchased 200 acres of land around Frinton, on the Essex coast, and employed the young architect Oliver Hill to design a housing estate featuring avant-garde designs, large windows and flat roofs for sunbathing. He invited designs from the leading architects working in the International Style, including Wells Coates, Frederick Gibberd, F.R.S. Yorke, and Amyas Connell, to designs sections of the scheme and work commenced on around 35 houses designed by Hill and local architects close to the sea. However, the buildings were clearly too daring for local tastes and by 1935 the company was nearly bankrupt and Hill resigned the post, leaving Frinton Park Estate today as a small but rare experiment in Modernist housing.*

scullery or washroom off it, was now incorporated within the main body of the house. Although still small by modern standards, the kitchen in Art Deco houses would have been a step up for most new owners used to cooking, eating and living in a cramped, old-fashioned living room.

LEADING ARCHITECTS

During the 18th and 19th centuries the role of the architect had developed from an amateur gentleman to a highly-respected professional controlling not only the design but also the many and often complex parts of the construction process. However, in the 20th century, the increasing variety in building types, materials and more demanding regulations encouraged many to form partnerships and to specialise, with fine houses built by these less well-known groups and local practices rather than the independent architects whose names stand out in history. There were some of note, however, who were at the forefront of design in Britain and introduced the Modern style to these shores, creating some of the most iconic buildings of the 1930s.

WELLS COATES

Wells Wintemute Coates, OBE, was a remarkably multi-talented Canadian architect who also designed Art Deco Bakelite radios, the 'D' handle for furniture, a microphone for the BBC, a catamaran and a monorail system – projects that were ahead of their time and, like his buildings, too daring for many. He was born in Japan in 1895 to Methodist missionary parents, studied for his degree in Canada after serving in the RAF during the First World War and moved to England in the 1920s. In 1928 he set up his own design business and was a co-founder of the Modern

FIG 2.12: LAWN ROAD FLATS, HAMPSTEAD, LONDON: *Designed by Wells Coates and Isokon in 1934 and intended to be the first word in modern design in this country. The building was aimed at the young professionals' market in London and comprised 29 apartments, along with staff accommodation, kitchens and a large garage. Although it remained a unique experiment in its day, it was successful in becoming the centre of intellectual social life in the area with Agatha Christie one of its residents and leading artists such as Barbara Hepworth, Ben Nicholson and Henry Moore visitors to its bar, which was added in 1937.*

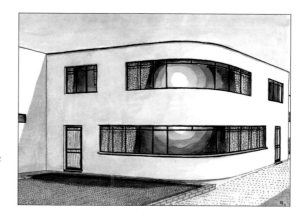

Fig 2.13: *The Sunspan House was designed by Wells Coates and Pleydell-Bouverie and is pictured here at the 1934 Ideal Home Exhibition, with furnishings supplied by Gordon Russell Ltd. The curved façade with elongated windows maximising sunlight is everything we associate with Art Deco but this modern design was too daring for most and only a few were ever built.*

Architectural Research Group (MARS). He employed his appreciation for Japanese simplicity in living spaces and for Le Corbusier's idea of a house being a machine to live in at his 1934 Lawn Road Flats in Hampstead (the Isokon Building). With its graceful white reinforced concrete walls, long cantilevered balconies and tower it was compared at the time to an ocean liner and featured a communal kitchen with meals dispatched up to the flats via dumb waiters! This experiment in modern living had central heating, hot water and built-in furniture, which Coates saw as an integral part of the design in each of the 29 apartments. He was also responsible for designing the Sunspan House with David Pleydell-Bouverie, with its distinctive curved glass windows designed to catch the maximum light. It featured at the 1934 Ideal Home Exhibition and although only a few of the design were ever built it is still distinctive of British Art Deco. Other projects included Embassy Court in Brighton and 10 Palace Gate, Kensington, in which he pioneered the idea of two principal rooms, one above the other, with high ceilings joined to lower bedrooms stacked three high, an ingenious 3:2 design that created spatial variation within a rectangular block. During the Second World War he helped with the design of fighter planes and for this work he later received the OBE. After the conflict he went on to plan new housing schemes, a monorail system and the Telekinema building for the Festival of Britain before his death in 1958.

AMYAS CONNELL

Amyas Douglas Connell was a pioneering architect who built one of the earliest Modernist houses in Britain but integrated elements of Classical architecture in his work. Born in New Zealand in 1901, he was brought up by his artistic parents in an area where new buildings using reinforced concrete were being erected. He combined this knowledge of concrete with his training at the hands of a leading Neo Classical architect before studying in Europe and setting up his office in London in 1929. Working with Stewart Lloyd Thompson he designed the first notable concrete Modernist house in Britain: High and Over in Amersham, Buckinghamshire. A large, white, Y-shaped structure dominating the hillside above the old Chiltern town, it caused quite a stir at the time within this strip

FIG 2.14: HIGH AND OVER, AMERSHAM, BUCKINGHAMSHIRE: *This daring design for the notable archaeologist Professor Bernard Ashmole was completed in 1931 by Connell and Thompson. Originally it was almost a small country house in scale, with its own water tower and generator set in landscaped gardens but these have now been encroached upon by later development.*

of respectability alongside the Metropolitan Railway, made famous by John Betjeman in his BBC documentary *Metro-land*. One of the problems with designing a house in reinforced concrete was that a largely conservative building industry had little experience in working with it, and the few large companies that did were not interested in such a small project (although High and Over was once branded as 'the last great country house'). Therefore Connell and Thompson had to change the design to one with a concrete load-bearing frame with brick and block-work walls. These were then rendered over to create the desired smooth, white finish. The innovative design and construction method was complemented by a quality interior with woods, marble and fittings that are still in good condition today and by a distinctive sun terrace along the top. Although upon its completion in 1931 it aroused mixed reactions, it was pivotal in introducing the style to a wider public. In 1933 Connell set up a practice with his brother-in-law Basil Ward and Colin Lucas. The partnership of Connell, Ward and Lucas produced a number of notable Modernist houses and flats in the years up to the Second World War before they went their

FIG 2.15: THE SUN HOUSES, AMERSHAM, BUCKINGHAMSHIRE: *One of a row of speculatively-built modern houses designed by Connell, Ward and Lucas on the road leading to High and Over between 1933–35.*

separate ways. Connell later designed buildings in Narobi, Kenya, before returning to Britain where he died in 1980.

FREDERICK GIBBERD

Sir Frederick Ernest Gibberd was one of the most prolific architects after the Second World War. He was responsible for numerous large-scale municipal schemes and housing projects, as well as notable buildings such as 'Paddy's Wigwam', the Liverpool Metropolitan Cathedral. However, he was also an innovative designer of modern flats in the 1930s. He was born in Coventry in 1908 and studied architecture in Birmingham, where he became friends with F.R.S. Yorke, and set up his own practice in 1930. His first major work was Pullman Court, Streatham Hill, London, completed in 1936. It was a white Modernist complex designed as affordable housing and was followed by further work at Park Court, Sydenham and Ellington Court, Southgate, both in London. He also collaborated with Yorke on the influential book *The Modern Flat*. It is his post-war output for which he will be best remembered, especially his work in the new town of Harlow where he also lived up until his death in 1984.

OLIVER HILL

Oliver Hill was a slightly eccentric and unconventional designer of large houses who not only baffled guests with unscheduled bouts of nudism but also architectural commentators in his swing from traditional to the modern and back again! Born in 1887, he was a family friend of Edwin Lutyens and began designing country houses and gardens in a style similar to the great architect. However, in the early 1930s, he became one of the leading exponents of Modernism in this country, embracing the constructional possibilities of concrete, the fanciful geometric and streamlined shapes it could create and the mix of textures in modern materials. He designed the iconic Midland Hotel in Morecambe, with its distinctive sweeping, streamlined profile, for the London Midland & Scottish Railway Company. He also worked on a number of large houses including his most notable, Landfall in Poole, and was responsible for the design

FIG 2.16: THE MIDLAND HOTEL, MORECAMBE, LANCASHIRE: *With the Depression of the late 1920s the wealthy could no longer afford foreign holidays so to attract this class of client the Midland Railway commissioned Hill to design this most modern of hotels, which opened its doors to great acclaim in 1933.*

**FIG 2.17:
FRINTON,
ESSEX:** *The
Round House
designed by
Hill featured
a plan of the
Frinton Park
Estate in the
floor within.*

of one of the only large-scale estates in a modern style at Frinton, Essex (see Fig 2.11). He was less productive after the Second World War and returned to more traditional styles in his later work before his death in 1968.

BERTHOLD LUBETKIN

Berthold Romanovich Lubetkin was one of the most radical architects working in Britain during the 1930s and 40s. He not only created notable modern houses and flats fitted with the latest features but also made them available to everyone. He was born in 1901 in Georgia, and developed his architectural skills firstly in Moscow where he was influenced by Constructivism and then in Paris where he established his first practice and came into contact with some of the leading designers, such as Le Corbusier. He moved to London in 1931 and, in the following year, along with other radical young architects who shared his views, he founded the architectural group Tecton (shortened from 'architecton', the Greek word for architecture). They were responsible for buildings at London, Whipsnade and Dudley zoos where they had a free hand to demonstrate the constructional possibilities of concrete and the graceful simplicity of their curving, white structures. Another project was Highpoint 1 in Highgate, a seven-storey block of flats raised up on columns with white concrete walls and balconies, built for them by Ove Arup (founder of Arup, the world-famous design and engineering consultants) who worked closely for the group on their projects. They were responsible for the only Modernist terrace built at the time, in Plumstead. Lubetkin also designed a unique house in Gidea Park, which was used by Kellogg's on cereal packets to represent the sunshine house for modern living. Despite his Communist and Modernist ideals that these buildings should be classless, they were nearly all snapped up by the wealthy middle classes and still today command a high price.

His most notable work was for Finsbury Council for whom he designed a much acclaimed health centre in 1938, which was available for all to use ten years before the NHS was established, and a series of flats in the post-war period fitted with lifts and central heating, the first of which, Spa Green, has now been Grade II* listed. However, in the latter part of his career, he became disillusioned with the authorities. He quit as the architect of Peterlee New Town when it became clear they were not going to build his dream of a miners' capital for the working men he greatly admired. His more decorative and inventive form of Modernism was replaced by the brutal looking high rise blocks that gave the movement such a bad reputation in this country. He spent his last years in Bristol, a city he saw as a home of scientific and engineering excellence, which was what first attracted him to Britain, and he campaigned to preserve the views of Brunel's Clifton Suspension Bridge. Since his death in 1990 his work in the decades either side of the Second World War has been rightly appreciated as examples of what might have been, and a theatre in Peterlee and a series of lectures by the Royal Institute of British Architects have been named in his memory.

FIG 2.18: *The rather austere, white-painted concrete walls of this L-shaped house disguise the attractive and private garden area at the rear. It was a prize-winning entry by Tecton in the Gidea Park Modern Homes Exhibition of 1934 and is now Grade II listed (the porch on the right is a modern addition).*

THOMAS TAIT

Thomas Smith Tait was already an established architect when, in the 1920s, he became one of the first to design houses in a Modern style, including an outstanding estate for workers of Crittall, the metal window-frame manufacturer. He was born in Paisley in 1882 and for most of his career worked for the notable architect Sir John James Burnet. In 1930 the practice changed its name to Burnet, Tait and Lorne and became one of the leading architectural firms in the following decade. Tait's work includes the pylons for the Sydney Harbour Bridge (the tall masonry supports at each end), a number of offices and hospitals, and work on Selfridges, Oxford Street. He was also the judge who chose the final design for the De La Warr Pavilion in Bexhill-on-Sea. He designed a number of notable Modern houses from the late 1920s, some

FIG 2.19: HAMILTON TERRACE, MAIDA VALE, LONDON: *This characteristic Art Deco semi was built for the Marques and Marquesa de Casa Maury by Tait and completed in 1938.*

FIG 2.20: LE CHATEAU, SILVER END, ESSEX: *One of the most notable developments influenced by the International Style was at Silver End, designed by Tait for the Crittall window company. It remains a unique example of workers' housing built in a modern style during this period (see also Chapter 3). Part of the scheme was three detached houses for the managers, including this example, which is also by Tait.*

with distinctive curved Art Deco features, others were more notably Modernist. The workers' estate houses at Silver End, Essex are probably his most unique and striking contribution to the style and they are still standing today in their original form. He was responsible for much of the design of the Empire Exhibition in Glasgow in 1938 and worked during the war as Director of Standardisation in the Ministry of Works before his death in 1954.

F.R.S. YORKE

Francis Reginald Stevens Yorke was as prolific and influential with his writing on modern architecture as he was in actually practising it. After the Second World War, his work and knowledge of the new materials required to rebuild cash-strapped Britain was an inspiration and the source of a successful business. The son of an architect, he was born in 1906 in Stratford-upon-Avon and came into contact with many of the leading European designers while writing articles for the *Architects' Journal*. This familiarity with their work was the foundation of a series of highly influential books that he published in the 1930s, introducing Modernist ideas and the use of new materials in domestic building to a still conservative trade; *The Modern House,* published in 1934, and *The Modern House in England*, published in 1937, being perhaps the most notable. He was also a founder member of the MARS group and worked with Marcel Breuer from the Bauhaus when he fled Germany after the Nazis' rise to power in 1933. He only produced a few buildings during this time, his first in 1934 being a fine example of the modern style he preached although he was still equally happy working with a more traditional English palette on a few of his projects. In 1944 he founded a new practice with Eugene Rosenberg and Cyril

FIG 2.21: SEA LANE HOUSE, EAST PRESTON, SUSSEX: *This distinctive house was designed by Marcel Breuer and F.R.S. Yorke and was completed in 1937.*

FIG 2.22: TORILLA, HATFIELD, HERTFORDSHIRE: *F.R.S. Yorke's first Modernist house, completed in 1935, built of concrete and later covered in render, with a notable two-storey living room. The large first-floor window was made by Lenscrete, a company who were notable at the time for producing glass lenses set in concrete and glass bricks that were used for staircase windows, skylights and pavement lights.*

Mardall. Together they went on to design a wide range of projects, including schools and colleges, for which Yorke was mainly responsible, and large schemes like St Thomas's Hospital and Gatwick Airport before his death in 1962.

Despite the advantages these buildings had with their concrete structure creating flexibility and freedom of interior space, they were still seen by many people as too impractical for this climate and clashing violently with their surroundings. It is not surprising that most were therefore built in London where there was a very cosmopolitan client base and along the south-east coast where the buildings' white façades fitted in better with the seaside location. As they were often weekend retreats, owners were less concerned about their rather harsh appearance. Although it would be after the war that the ability to construct these types of houses cheaper en masse, using materials that were readily available, made them the answer to the housing shortage, they did have some influence on the speculatively-built estates in the 1930s. In the next chapter we look at how these, combined with the strong influence of American modern design, helped to create a style of house that is distinctly Art Deco.

FIG 2.23: *Examples of large houses built by other less well known architects and partnerships in the International Style. They were not only daring in their appearance but inventive in the internal arrangement, often with sliding partitions to turn living areas into a larger or sub-divided space. The houses featured so far would mostly have been commissioned and hence could be adapted for the owner's taste and expected use. However, the next chapter looks at speculatively-built homes in which the structure remained fairly fixed but to which details made popular by these architects could be applied, creating the familiar semi-detached Art Deco house.*

CHAPTER 3

FIG 3.1: *Probably the most recognisable face of Art Deco housing is the Moderne semi, a softened version of the International Style, which still form substantial parts of 1930s' estates today.*

ART DECO HOUSING

Semis, Flats and Workers' Estate Houses

Suburbia

If the Victorian rush to the cities had been largely absorbed by tightly-packed terraced housing wrapped around old urban centres, then the inter-war shift of population to the capital and new industrial centres was characterised by the semis. These distinctive stout buildings, with their spacious plot of land, spread in an uncontrolled wave across the countryside, turning fields and old country estates into suburbia. Most of the impetus was created by those seeking jobs in the new light industries mainly in the Midlands and South but especially in London, which saw its population grow by around a million in only a decade.

The creation of the suburbs to absorb this rapid influx (or at least to house those who wanted to move out of the city centre, making their old homes available for newcomers) was only possible because land was very cheap. This was due to the after effects of the agricultural depression and the selling off of country estates now that the gentry, crippled by land and hereditary taxes, had also lost their heirs in the First World War. An acre of building land could cost as little as a few hundred pounds in 1920 and

FIG 3.2: *Moderne semis, with distinctive curved sun-trap windows, white-rendered brick walls and concrete semi-circular porches. Despite the appearance of the International Style the structure was identical to others on the estate in a Mock Tudor style; this was only a veneer of modernity.*

Fig 3.3: *These houses built in 1935 were designed by Douglas Wood Architects and were part of an exclusive development laid out to the north of the new underground station at Stanmore, North London.*

although it more than doubled in price by 1939 it was still a very small proportion of the overall costs. The other principal reason the suburbs grew was the development of a transport network. In the 1800s most people walked to work so housing naturally squeezed itself in as close to the sources of employment as possible. By the turn of the 20th century, however, the bicycle, tram and cheaper train tickets had made commuting affordable for the masses and ignited the spread of suburbia. By the 1930s the growth of car ownership and creation of new main roads attracted ribbons of development along them. In London it was the spread of new underground lines that was the major factor in determining where houses were built, some developers snapping up land around stations even before the lines had been constructed.

The demand for housing immediately after the First World War had been created by returning soldiers expecting an improved standard of living after risking their lives for their country. Fearful of the sort of revolution that had gripped Russia, the Government sought to provide 'Homes Fit For Heroes'. This short-lived scheme was economically impossible and was wound up after a few years with the Government looking to the private sector to drive the house-building boom by offering them fixed subsidies. Previously, most housing had been erected by small-scale builders usually constructing a short row of homes, and selling or renting them out, before moving on to the next part of the road. After the First World War, however, the boom in housing created the opportunity for builders to expand and establish some of the large-scale construction companies with which we are familiar today.

Although land was cheap and there were few restrictions that would cost the builder much money, the price of materials was still high due to post-war shortages. Despite attempts at state ownership of brickworks and timber yards, the cost of building a house actually increased during the 1920s, while experiments with more economic forms of housing and the use of concrete, iron and steel had little effect on buyers who still preferred traditional brick structures. It was only when the timber, bricks and fittings were able to be bought en masse by the new larger private building companies and local authorities that the price of a house was reduced. Falling prices meant that by the mid 1930s the cost of the cheapest properties had dropped by nearly half, to approximately £400. This was still a lot of money at the time so the Government not only aided the construction industry but provided building societies with tax concessions to enable them to offer mortgages on more competitive terms. Thus, by the 1930s, down payments of as little as £5 could secure you a home, and weekly repayments from around 10 shillings (50p) encouraged the shift from a population that mainly rented to one of largely owner occupiers by the late 1980s.

Council and Workers' Estates

Before the First World War the Victorian doctrine of self-help meant that the authorities only reluctantly became involved in providing housing for the poorest in society and most of the schemes that had been developed offering homes to

FIG 3.4: *A mock-up of a typical advert for houses in the 1930s, with the emphasis on health and sunshine at a low rate of payment.*

FIG 3.5: *A contemporary advert for houses built for the Metropolitan Railway as they developed the land adjoining their new stations.*

the working classes were private ventures. In the aftermath of the war, however, attitudes changed and with financial incentives from the Government, local councils began to build houses with the intention of clearing the worst of the inner-city slums. Most were erected on cheap suburban land, with Becontree in East London being the largest housing estate in Europe at the time. Some had their own railway line to bring imported materials onto site, whilst others were smaller, with semis and short rows of terraces set in attractive tree-lined streets inspired by the Garden City movement from the turn of the century. As a result of the high building costs, large plots and types of house built, these first council estates were still rather expensive for tenants to rent and it was often only the better-off workers who could afford to live there. There was something of a down market exclusivity about them, reinforced by inspectors who made regular visits to make sure the strict rules on maintenance and behaviour were being adhered to. However, despite the fact that they were now living in spacious homes with hot water, electricity and their own toilet, many tenants found themselves miles away from their families and with the high cost of rent they fled back to their old cramped homes!

Despite the advantages that new materials and Modernist designs could potentially provide in cutting the costs of housing for the poor, there were only a few estates of non traditional housing built before the Second World War. Most were designed along the lines of an Arts and Crafts cottage or Neo Georgian house, usually with tall, hipped

FIG 3.6: SILVER END, ESSEX: *In April 1926 Francis Henry Crittall, the owner of Crittall Windows, started building a housing estate for his workers next to the new factory he established between Braintree and Witham. The houses were in a modern style with flat roofs and his own metal-framed windows (see also Fig 2.20). Over 150 were completed by the time the Depression at the end of the decade reduced Crittall's originally grander scheme. Today they still stand as a unique and well-preserved example of a modern style workers' estate.*

roofs and a few bits of decorative moulding in the form of projecting bricks above and below windows and a simple porch. These estates came in for much criticism from those campaigning to clear the still appalling slum conditions within which a large proportion of the population were still trapped. The estates were seen as a backward and expensive option and many advocated the approach taken on the Continent where apartments with hot and cold water, bathrooms and central heating were being built. It was thought that flats would provide a more economic solution to the problem but it was not until after the Second World War that this was attempted on a large scale.

Flats

FIG 3.7: *Apartment blocks from North London that have retained their original Art Deco railings, glazed pantiles and green and white colour scheme.*

In the 1920s and 30s, flats were still something of an exclusive form of housing. Low-rise blocks had been built in the late Victorian period: a few brutally plain types for the working classes in a number of cities and, more typically, so-called mansions, smart red brick apartments surrounded by gardens in the better-off areas. In the inter-war years these private apartments became a popular option for cosmopolitan and business types and they sprang up in many major towns and cities, but especially in London and

FIG 3.8: *Examples of Art Deco flats finished in brick or white render. Note the use of curved windows, green pantiles and a stepped monumental entrance (bottom left), which are distinctive of this period.*

also along the coast in seaside resorts. It is perhaps on this form of building rather than conventional housing that the Art Deco style can be more readily found today.

Although some complexes like Highpoint and Lawn Road Flats mentioned in the previous chapter had encapsulated the Modernist ideals through the entire structure, the more numerous speculatively-built, low-rise blocks were usually conventional apartments with little invention in their internal planning and just a Moderne cloak covering the exterior. Many had plain brick or white rendered walls, pitched roofs covered in the 1930s by glossy green glazed pantiles, balconies with curved ends and steel rods or striking geometric patterned railings, a monumental style communal entrance and smart, laid out gardens often featuring exotic plants.

The Semi

High-rise living and the thought of being tightly packed into small apartments was still alien to most people in this country, so of the approximately four million homes built during the inter-war years, the majority were three-bed semis. These suburban properties provided their new owners with a front and back garden, gas and electricity laid on, hot and cold running water, a bathroom with a flushing toilet next to it, and a driveway for some. A distinctive feature of these semi-detached houses was to have the front doors set on the outer edges of the pair rather than next to each other in the centre as had been the norm before the First World War; this increased the feeling of privacy for the owner. The hall was wider in most standard housing, compared with Edwardian houses. This extra space meant that the stairs could be brought to the front of the house, with decorative balustrades, rather than being squashed in at the rear or trapped in the middle between dividing walls. Rear extensions for service rooms and storage, which had been a standard feature of Victorian and Edwardian houses, were now gone; the kitchen, larder and coal store were built within the stout body of the house, with a dining room and living room downstairs and three bedrooms upstairs being the most common arrangement.

As margins became tight and competition vigorous, speculative builders could not afford to have properties standing unoccupied for long. Not only did they offer houses with inducements like extra fittings, new appliances or financial offers, they also

FIG 3.9: *Examples of Moderne semis and detached suburban houses with distinctive curved and corner windows, hipped roofs and concrete slab porches.*

FIG 3.10: *Examples of suburban houses built in the International Style with flat roofs, a strong horizontal emphasis and rectangular in form. Some were little more than a conventional semi (top left) but others had more inventive layouts.*

FIG 3.11: *Many houses built in this period had eclectic mixes of styles. This example has a Moderne green-tiled roof and corner windows but although the stepped gable at the front is Art Deco in form it looks as if it was inspired by a Scottish castle!*

made sure they were built in a style that would attract buyers. For most this meant brick structures with a large square or semi-circular bay window, a bit of fake timber-framing and a steep hipped roof. It was only the more adventurous company who would build in a Modern style and only then in areas like London and coastal resorts where they knew they were more readily accepted.

The distinctive form of house that we know as Art Deco today was mostly a watered down version of Jazz Moderne, Streamline and Hollywood style, placed upon the standard semi-detached or detached structure and often with elements from a number of styles mixed up in one design. Some had curved ends to bays, concrete slab porches, steel-framed windows, and rendered brick surface painted white, with perhaps a few horizontal bands or geometric pattern breaking up the surface. Builders would often offer the house with a flat roof hidden behind a low parapet or railing, but despite being cheaper most buyers paid extra to have a conventional hipped roof built or had one fitted later. Bright green paintwork and colourful splashes of glass in the door and windows made these houses stand out from the traditional crowd around them and created a little oasis of exotic modernity amongst their more conservative neighbours.

FIG 3.12: *It is not uncommon to find a few houses on 1930s' estates that still have their original windows and doors. Although estate agents often recommend owners to put in UPVC windows, as this can give a temporary lift in value, they often spoil the appearance and need replacing after a decade or two (think how out of date 1980s' aluminium windows now look). Original metal-framed windows last much longer and, with their horizontal lines, fit in with the style of house and add to its long-term value. However, they do require maintenance and will need secondary glazing fitting inside if noise is a problem. There are a number of companies now producing authentic 1930s' style double-glazed windows and they are worth looking up on the internet.*

CHAPTER 4

FIG 4.1: *The Art Deco themes of bold, colourful designs and horizontal and geometric patterns are clearly evident in the limited but distinctive windows, doors and decorative fittings applied to houses.*

ART DECO DETAILS

Doors, Windows and Decoration

Although the plain white and curving walls of Art Deco houses make their form distinctive, there were also unique characteristics to the fittings built into them. The windows, doors and porches were often the only part of the façade where the bold geometric patterns that so distinguish the style were found. These details were also more widely available than before, as their simple forms could easily be mass-produced while many parts on cheaper housing were imported in bulk from countries like Czechoslovakia to further reduce costs. Due to the effect these fittings had in creating a strong horizontal emphasis or distinguishing an otherwise plain façade they are important for maintaining the Art Deco character of the house and their removal can have a more destructive effect than on earlier houses. This chapter shows what the original windows, doors and decorative fittings would have looked like and so help in identifying the style, finding suitable parts when restoring a house and deciding the worth of keeping those that are still in situ.

FIG 4.2: *The chevron pattern was one of the most distinctive features of metal-framed windows. These had been developed and manufactured by Crittall, a company established in 1849 but which, under the founder's son F.H. Crittall, rapidly expanded in the decades before the First World War, specialising in the production of metal-framed windows which were fitted, amongst other places, on the* Titanic! *During the 1920s and 30s their steel frames became widely used, in part due to the metal's strength, which meant the bars could be much thinner than other materials so increasing the area of glass and the ease by which it could be formed into a curved profile, but also because they were cheaper than many other types and with regular painting could last for generations. (There are now companies that can be located via the internet who will make authentic replacement metal-framed windows, which are 'A-rated', if the originals are beyond repair.)*

FIG 4.3: *Examples of Crittall-type windows, many with the distinctive curved sun-trap.*

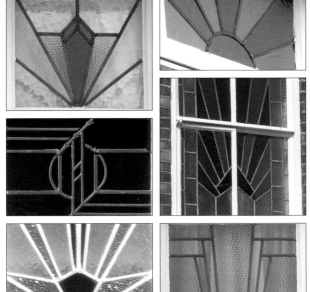

FIG 4.4: *Bold geometric patterns in the tops of casement windows were characteristic of Art Deco houses, some using strong colours, others different textures of glass (above), this latter type being very distinctive of 1930s' windows.*

Fig 4.5: *The most characteristic emblem of 1930s' housing was the sun-ray pattern; the radiating lines can be found on gable ends, gates and, as in this example, glass panels. It is worth noting that fittings were just as likely to be changed in the past as they are today and you can often find a Victorian house with Art Deco-style glass in its windows as its owners tried to modernise the property, so do not take the use of these patterns on its own as a dating tool.*

Fig 4.6: *Windows that cut through the corner of a house, thin vertical openings with stepped bases to match the staircase they illuminated and portholes usually close to doors are all characteristic of Art Deco houses.*

FIG 4.7: *Exterior doors were generally simple on Moderne houses, with vertical geometric patterns and textured glass the most common form. Originally most would have been painted dark colours (bottom left), yellow was more popular in the 1950s and white only practical in the cleaner recent decades.*

FIG 4.8: *Porches were often no more than a slab of reinforced concrete (or a covered wooden frame) cantilevered out from the face of the house on Art Deco houses.*

Fig 4.9: *The 1920s' fashion for all things Egyptian or Aztec was apparent around the door where monumental surrounds inspired by buildings from the Ancient World were often fitted.*

Fig 4.10: *Conventional doors could have Art Deco-style patterns inserted, as on this example. Letterboxes were also characteristically geometric in form with shallow pointed tops, stepped edges and a chromium finish (for handles see Chapter 5).*

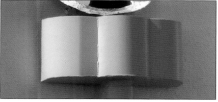

Fig 4.11: *Guttering could be prominent on the exterior of Moderne houses. Rainwater traps were usually decorated, either with angular designs or simple curving forms, as in these two examples.*

FIG 4.12: *Railings and gates were often decorated with distinctive geometric patterns, which are a key part of the style and character of the building. Some were simply horizontally-set steel rods, others more elaborate designs originally painted in strong colours such as vivid green or black.*

FIG 4.13: *Although the most ardent Modernist supporters would have pulled their hair out when they saw plain white walls being decorated with patterns, most speculative builders knew that their clients would want the extremely plain façade broken up by more homely features. Some had bold horizontal bands raised above the surface (right), others had patterns set in the render – wavy lines, geometric designs or coloured tiles (left)*

FIG 4.14: *The theme of celebrating the sun was represented on the exterior of Art Deco houses with balconies, as in this example (right), behind characteristic horizontal railings or sun lounges on the roof hidden behind a solid wall parapet, sometimes with a glass room and concrete slab cover.*

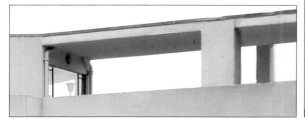

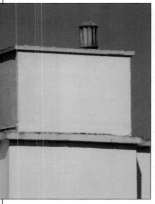

FIG 4.15: *Chimneys, which had been a major decorative feature on late Victorian houses, were hidden from view on Moderne houses where practicable as they did not fit in with the ideal of a modern, clean and sunlit home. By the 1930s, houses were being fitted with fewer fireplaces – there might have been a chimney only for the living room fire and kitchen boiler – and in the most modern flats none at all.*

Art Deco houses are only now being appreciated for their distinct period character and the fittings illustrated above should be preserved where they survive; there is no doubt that the value of original properties will increase as the style grows in popularity. This is helped by their unique appearance and in many areas their relative rarity; in my home town of Leek there is only one Moderne pair of semis left amongst the hundreds that were built in the period. However, this total style with its shocking modern geometric forms was more readily accepted in the interior and now we must step beyond the front door and see how the rooms inside would have appeared in the inter-war house.

CHAPTER 5

FIG 5.1: *Boxy settees, beige tiled fireplaces and geometric-shaped pelmets above curtains were some of the distinctive elements of Art Deco interiors, as in this bold example.*

ART DECO INTERIORS

Rooms, Decoration and Fittings

Art Deco interiors are a familiar image from film and television, with luxurious ocean liners, the Orient Express, fashionable hotels and exclusive apartments featuring in adaptations of books such as the *Poirot* series. They are exotic and modern, spacious and bright, with patterned glossy wood furniture, chromium and plywood chairs, large expanses of mirrors and glass, and splashes of geometric patterns and stylised figurines. They offer bold, stylish and exciting surroundings in complete contrast to the dark, cluttered and busy interiors we associate with the Victorian period.

Yet, despite the widespread availability of this total style and the existence of a few fully-fitted examples in premium houses, commercial buildings and exclusive flats, it is debatable how many complete Art Deco interiors could be found at the time in the British home. Although some of the young and cosmopolitan types would have welcomed this fresh, new style, most householders were more restrained and traditional,

FIG 5.2: *Home owners could gain inspiration from a number of new magazines displaying the latest fashions in interior design, such as* Ideal Home. *Here is a distinctive Art Deco living room featuring geometric-patterned fabrics and rug, box-shaped chairs, stepped fireplace and metal-framed French doors.*

still organising their house like their Victorian predecessors, albeit with a lighter and more open feel. Modernist architects showed what was possible as concrete freed the interior from load-bearing walls and introduced the open plan; yet most in the country still desired a parlour – an enclosed room with the best furniture reserved for special occasions.

Although a lucky few made a fortune in this period, most suffered some effects from the economic problems that blighted the inter-war years. Those who benefited from jobs in the new industries were often stretching their finances in order to buy a house so the fixtures and fittings within might be a mix of hand-me-downs, renovated bargains and a few new pieces where required. Numerous magazines and books were published showing the owner how to make furniture, tackle small building jobs, and redecorate the house. There were limitations on what could be done, however, as in these years before the DIY craze there was not the wide range of products available that there is today. For instance, there were no colour charts for the limited range of ready-mixed coloured paints; most people still used professionals who mixed their own colours when it came to redecorating. Although the theme of the period was light and sunshine, with large windows and brighter colours freshening the interior, most owners still had heating provided by coal fires, so furnishings, walls and floors would have patterns, grained effects or mottled finishes to disguise the dirt.

This chapter will show the fixtures and fittings that could be found at the time in the British home – to help those who are renovating or creating an Art Deco interior to recognise the pieces and put together a design. If, however, you are trying to understand

FIG 5.3: *In the more modest semi-detached house there was still scope for Art Deco fixtures and fittings. However, most families would not have been able to afford a complete makeover so furniture was bought one piece at a time to make a more eclectic collection, as in this example.*

what the inside of a house looked like at the time, it is important to remember that although some pieces such as radios, settees and mirrors were widely accepted in a modern style it is likely that most people mixed them with older traditional pieces, due to budget or taste. The change from the dark and busy Victorian interior, with numerous rooms allocated to a specific role and a marked division between family and servants' quarters, to one of light, spacious and more open planning, with modern appliances integrated within the home, would take a number of generations and to some extent has never been completely adopted.

FIG 5.4: *American born Marion Dorn moved to London in 1923, where she established herself as one of the leading designers of fabrics and carpets, with her textiles appearing in leading hotels like the Savoy, Claridge's and the Midland Hotel, Morecambe (see Fig 2.16). She produced modern designs for Wilton rugs (right), established her own company in 1934 and gained commissions for the* Queen Mary *liner and fabrics for underground trains.*

Art Deco Interiors

The epitome of the style is seen in the luxurious interiors created by leading architects and designers for hotels, ocean liners, offices and the finest homes. Some made use of glossy and reflective surfaces to create vibrant new schemes, with silver and bronze metalwork and the natural grain of the wood put on show (this reflected the honesty in design whereby materials used were left in their natural state and not painted or grained to look like something else, which had been typical of Victorian interiors). Others were Modernist, with bright rooms lit by windows that filled a wall and minimalistic furniture and fittings. Whichever form they took, these Art Deco interiors were linked by the use of modern materials – chromium, mirrors, glass and plywood. Stylish chairs by Alvar Aalto or Jack Pritchard, furniture by Betty Joel and Arundell Clarke and rugs by Marion Dorn were fitted within the most exclusive properties, while those wishing to emulate the finest interiors seen in magazines such as *House and Garden* or *Ideal Home* could shop at Heal's, one of the few outlets where modern furniture and fittings were available, or visit exclusive collections such as Curtis Moffat's gallery in Fitzroy Square, London.

FIG 5.5: *The daughter of the British diplomat and art collector Sir James Stewart Lockhart, Betty Joel, was brought up in the Far East and combined the simple designs from here with the ethics of Arts and Crafts when she began designing furnishings and fabrics in England from 1921. She produced pieces for a wealthy clientele but was practical and commercially astute in her approach and many of her designs were copied for the mass market. Her early furniture tends to be more traditional in inspiration but by the 1930s she was creating designs with curved elements and modern materials, a popular blend of old and new. In addition to furniture, she designed fabrics, rugs, theatre sets, radio cabinets and even kitchen stoves, before she stepped back from work in 1937 while her husband, David Joel, continued the business (his naval background had meant that the couple had an understanding of boat building techniques, which was useful in designing furniture with curved shapes and laminated woods as used on the dresser pictured here).*

FIG 5.6: *One of the leading designers of steel-framed and plywood furniture in Britain during the 1930s, Jack Pritchard was key in introducing the modern style in this country. Seeing the opportunity for functional designed furnishings while he was marketing manager at Venesta, a manufacturer of new plywood goods, he produced his own designs, received commissions from leading architects such as Walter Gropius and Marcel Breuer and helped form Isokon, along with his colleague Wells Coates (see Chapter 2). The bookcase pictured here was designed by Egon Riss and Pritchard while he was in charge of Isokon in the late 1930s.*

The Rooms

With the larger plots available on cheaper suburban land the entrance to even the most modest house was more spacious than before. Larger detached properties were usually approached from under a porch or loggia, most recessed within the building but those on modern houses often having a projecting concrete slab, with simplified or smaller versions on semis. The hall was wider than most before the First World War, with a window to the side of the door rather than a fanlight above it now that the ceiling height in houses began to be reduced. The stairs were brought forward into this space, with a wooden balustrade up the side to make a more impressive display than was possible in the narrow Victorian house. It was still common for the hall to have a dado rail, though, with a painted or varnished embossed paper below so as not to show up the marks in this busy and often dirty part of the house.

In the larger modern house the old parlour or withdrawing room was replaced by a sizeable lounge or living room, one without a specific role unlike their 19th-century counterparts, and which hence had no set furniture or standard plan (the living room had formerly been a room in which everyday tasks like cooking and eating took place in smaller properties). However, most people still preferred to have separate rooms or a room reserved for special occasions. In more modest houses, therefore, there were always two main rooms, usually a living room at the front divided off from a small dining

FIG 5.7: *A hall from a semi-detached house, with Art Deco-style coloured glass in the door and window and a prominent staircase with a plain wooden rail and painted square profile balusters. In some of the more luxurious houses, ironwork painted to look like marble or spiral staircases was sometimes used (the spiral being a popular form with Modernists).*

FIG 5.8: *An example of an Art Deco living room with distinctive zigzag and wavy patterns on the furnishings. Note the patterned section of the wall framing the fireplace, a popular feature in magazines but less so in the ordinary home.*

room at the back. This latter space often made use of drop-down-leaf tables and limited furniture due to its more compact dimensions, while in larger houses the dining room remained reserved for meals and special occasions and could also be used as a quiet space for working where a separate study was not provided.

The inter-war kitchen represented a major change in domestic planning in this period now that servants were so hard to come by. Rather than having separate spaces for cooking and washing-up in the service end of the Victorian house, the 1920s' home now had the two combined into one modern room containing a sink, cooker, hot water boiler, storage, worktops and a small table with an enamelled top (larger houses might still have a separate room, referred to as a washroom or scullery, for doing the laundry). It was the first room of

FIG 5.9: *Modern architects tried to tear the focus of the room away from the fireplace, often using wall-mounted electric fires with no surrounds and creating large expanses of glass to fill a wall. In most houses, however, tradition reigned as in this example with a picture rail and chairs facing the fireplace. Despite the popularity of radio, a piano was still common.*

FIG 5.10: *An Art Deco dining room with striking lights, pelmet and fireplace, while the serving hatch was a modern feature that did not become common until the 1950s. In most houses, however, the dining room, as pictured here, was a rather compact area at the back of the house, often with French doors opening out into the garden. Flexible furniture like drop-down-leaf tables was useful for making the most of the space.*

the house in which built-in furniture became popular, although at this date it was still a luxury, with white-painted wooden base units in only the finest houses, while in more modest homes a tall utility cupboard with pull-down ironing board or pull-out table was a common fitting. In general the room still had a free-standing feel to it, with appliances and storage lining the walls, which were tiled on their lower half and oil painted above, with little consideration for ergonomics. As refrigerators were still rare at this date (people still had the time to shop daily for fresh food), most houses had a larder or pantry built off the kitchen although its position was less critical and the size often smaller than in older houses as tinned food became popular.

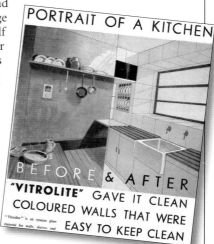

FIG 5.11: *Despite magazines and adverts picturing built-in kitchens, most still had a free-standing feel, with the furniture limited to a sink unit, as in this advert, and a tall utility cupboard. Duck egg blue, light green or just cream were popular colours.*

Upstairs the bedrooms were lighter in feel, partly helped by the widespread use of portable heaters or built-in electric fires, even where a fireplace had still been fitted. Families were happy to spend a large part of their income on good-quality bedroom furniture, with most having a suite containing a wardrobe, a chest of drawers, a tallboy for the gentleman and a large dressing table with triple frameless mirror for the ladies, while divan beds with a padded or wooden headboard became very popular in this period.

Easiwork *makes* *Britain's Kitchens up-to-date*

FIG 5.12: *Built-in kitchens like this example were limited to the most modern houses and apartments. However, the utility cupboard on the left was a common free-standing feature.*

FIG 5.13: *An Art Deco-style bedroom suite with a light coloured wood (triple mirrors on dressers were more usual than the single one shown here).*

FIG 5.14: *Although the furniture seems dark to modern eyes, woods like walnut were lighter than previous pieces. Some mixed up two different woods to create geometric patterns in the surface.*

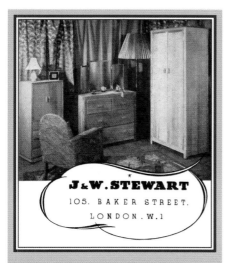

FIG 5.16: *The modern style was widely adopted in the bathroom irrespective of the exterior style, as in this rather luxurious example. Chrome was used for taps and fittings, baths were panelled in, there were plain glossy tiles and mirrors on the walls, and boxy pedestal wash-basins were common. In most houses, the toilet in the next room had a high level cistern, the best had new low-level silent ones.*

FIG 5.15: *An advert for a contemporary bedroom suite. As with most furniture it was generally boxy, some pieces having stepped crests or curved corners.*

The bathroom was small, with just a bath and hand-basin in most, tiles halfway up the walls and a painted surface above, and a separate water closet in an adjacent room. However humble this would look today, it was a major step up for many families who had previously had baths downstairs in front of the range or copper and had had to share toilet facilities with neighbours.

Decoration and Furnishings

Despite the influence of the leading designers of the age, the interior of most middle-class houses had to be more practical for everyday family life and reflect the more reserved nature of the owners. While the house was heated by coal fires, the interior surfaces had to be dark or patterned to disguise the dirt. As electric fires and portable heaters provided a cleaner atmosphere, so plain and light finishes and less elaborate window treatments became acceptable. Expensive pieces of furniture and fittings were likely to be in a plain colour, but the vibrant, colourful and geometric patterns of Art Deco were more readily accepted for decoration in the form of wallpaper, curtains and rugs – things that could be easily changed as fashions moved on. It was also usual to see items such as radios, vacuum cleaners and kitchen appliances shaped by the modern style while fireplaces, clocks and mirrors are some of the commonly seen pieces in Art Deco.

Most furniture in British homes was free-standing, notably close to the ground during this period rather than on high legs. Built-in pieces were not very popular except in some modern properties and apartments, despite being championed by leading architects. It is

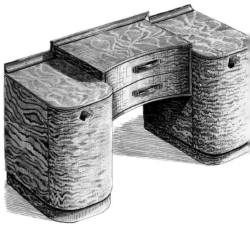

THE finest hardwoods, sound Craftsmanship, the last word in upholstery and coverings combine to give
MINTY CLUB CHAIRS a character of
their own. The patented unit construction enables the back and seat
to come away completely for cleaning
or loose covers.

The "MERTON"
From £3 . 19 . 6
According to Length of Seat.

SETTEE from £7 . 19 . 6
Write for Catalogue of the MINTY "COWLEY"
"MERTON" "LINCOLN" and "ISIS" Chairs and
patterns of coverings.

FIG 5.18: *Club chairs from Minty were typical of modern furniture in that they were boxy and close to the floor.*

FIG 5.17: *The finest Art Deco pieces from the 1920s were intricate examples of fine craftsmanship, with inlaid patterns using different woods and materials like ebony and ivory (above left). By the 1930s, however, the surfaces were plain and distinctive curved profiles became common (above right).*

in furniture that the first luxurious phase of Art Deco, that emanating in the mid 1920s, principally from France, is best seen. Every surface could be patterned by using the natural beauty of different and generally lighter woods and creating designs with marquetry, while the same care was taken with the fine details and in the overall design, which often incorporated clever swing-out or fold-over parts to make the item multi-purpose. These high-quality pieces of craftsmanship were affordable by only a select few and it was not until the 1930s that mass-produced modern furniture featuring curving fronts and corners, stepped features and plain lighter

FIG 5.19: *An Art Deco settee and chair with geometrical and chunky forms and low, wide backs and armrests. Another modern piece that was popular was the divan, a backless settee or chaise longue; the Vienna divan was curved upwards at both ends. Contrasting materials were sometimes used on upholstery, with leather and silk satin on some of the finest. In many homes loose covers were still common, usually with flecked or striped patterns to disguise the coal dust.*

woods began to make an impression within the average home. These distinctive pieces with oval or kidney shapes, Art Deco handles and settees and chairs with a chunky, square, box-like form are distinctive of the period.

Furnishing fabrics came in a wide variety of types, not only in the variety of patterns between traditional florals and modern geometric designs but also in the material itself. Leather, velvet and moquette (deep-piled, hard-wearing fabric, also used for upholstery on trains) and new synthetic products gave buyers greater choice. Early Art Deco designs followed the exotic theme with bright, colourful patterns; these were replaced in the 1930s by less vibrant

FIG 5.20: *A contemporary advert for occasional modern style furniture from the mid 1930s.*

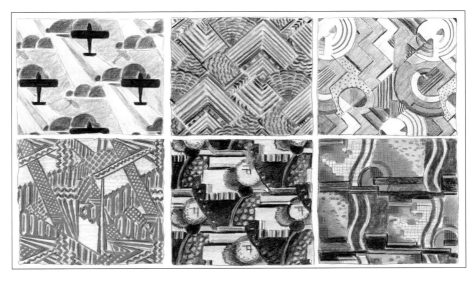

FIG 5.21: *Examples of Art Deco fabrics by leading designers of the time.*

maroons, browns and greens in plain or geometric designs. The traditional arrangement of multi layers of fabric covering the window began to change in this period, although frilly valances and nets were still widely used, with new materials like viscose rayon replacing traditional laces and muslin. In Art Deco interiors a geometric-designed pelmet with a simple curtain arrangement was popular; in some of the most modern, a plain opening with a venetian blind or just patterned or opaque glass in bathrooms was seen as sufficient.

Fitted carpets were still a luxurious

FIG 5.22: *A wide range of floor coverings were available in the 1930s, like this cord covering formed into colourful patterns and checks.*

rarity; most had either linoleum, which could be patterned to look like marble, a carpet piece (often flowered in the bedroom) or they had painted or stained floorboards with rugs spread over them.

The days of high ceilings with elaborate cornices and roses were left behind by the 1930s and in most inter-war properties the room height was lower and the surface was plain and painted with a white distemper. The walls below could be bare in the most modern property but were often broken up by a picture rail in suburban estates. Paints for walls could be durable oil-based matt, eggshell and gloss or distemper, which was still popular and cheaper, with a wider range of colours: ivory, coral, terracotta, geranium red, emerald and celadon green were common choices (blue greys were popular for floorboards in more modern schemes). Mottling, combing and scumbling treatments could be used to add texture and hide the dirt where there was still a coal fire.

FIG 5.23: *Parquet or imitation tiles were popular in halls and living rooms, while linoleum designed to look like a carpet could be used in dining rooms. Modern designs on linoleum, as in this example, were introduced in the 1930s.*

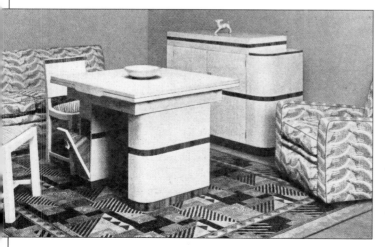

FIG 5.24: *Rugs were seen as more hygienic than fitted carpets as they could be shaken outside (they were also cheaper). Modern designs, as in this example, could be found in the most up-to-date interiors, with the exposed floorboards around it painted, grained or covered in linoleum.*

FIG 5.25: *Examples of wallpapers with Art Deco designs. Exotic patterns were popular in the 1920s, using the strong colours of red, blue and green. Tones were more muted in the 1930s, with beige, oranges, reds, browns, pinks, blues and greys being popular colours.*

Wallpaper was available with floral and foliage designs but geometric patterns grew in popularity, from the traditional tartan patterns to more modern designs, while embossed papers remained in widespread use in the suburbs. The interior woodwork was usually painted a flat stone colour or grained on top of this, a pattern imitating a high-quality wood, something that would never be done in a Modernist home. Internal doors could have a similar traditional treatment but painting them with two contrasting tones or colour combinations was very popular.

FIG 5.26: *Books and magazines began to show the public how they could decorate rooms themselves, as in this example demonstrating distempering and wallpapering.*

Fixtures and Fittings

For all the modernity that could be found inside the 1930s' home it seems strange that a coal fire was still the main source of heat in the principal rooms. Although the mechanics of the grate had changed little since the Late Victorian period, the fireplace had. It didn't matter what the external style of the house was, the old-fashioned wooden or stone surround, with recessed tiled inserts, was replaced by plain, modern-looking pieces with

DORATE YOUR OWN HOME WE'LL TELL YOU HOW

WOMAN'S OWN

2d.

FIG 5.27: *A selection of new women's magazines were also keen to show how to redecorate the interior.*

free-standing solid fuel boiler, which would provide hot water for the house and give off enough heat to keep the room warm. It would often have a tall, thin chimney on the back corner of hipped roofs to serve it although these became rather precarious and were later removed.

However, the days of the coal fire were numbered. Blocks of flats and some of the most modern houses had no chimneys and electric panel heaters or crude central heating systems with bulky radiators were fitted instead of a fireplace. The relatively low price of electricity now made this form of heating cost effective although it would be gas-fired boilers connected to central heating systems that would finally replace solid fuel heating in the late 1960s.

If electricity was only just starting to revolutionise interior heating, then it had already transformed the way the home was

no frame but a stepped profile made up of large glazed blocks or covered in tiles in distinctive creams, beiges and browns. There was always a fireplace in the lounge or living room, and there may have been one in other rooms but, increasingly, portable gas or electric heaters were used, especially in bedrooms. In the kitchen the old-fashioned range was being replaced in suburban properties by a gas cooker and a

FIG 5.28: *An advert for a fireplace in a distinctive Art Deco form. Some were covered in glazed tiles, others were made from large glazed blocks, as in this example, which could be shaped into curves and have bands of horizontal decoration (note the modern rug and clock).*

This fire gives you proved **economy** in a perfect setting

'THE **DEVON** FIRE"

FIG 5.29: *Examples of contemporary Art Deco fireplaces. Most were plain with stepped forms (bottom right examples) and decoration usually limited to horizontal bands (top left examples) and staggered sides to the fire grate (top right examples).*

FIG 5.30: *An advert for portable electric heaters, which were popular in upstairs rooms.*

lit. Although electric lighting was standard now in new houses, it was still a relatively new science and manufacturers were constantly improving the performance of the light bulb and producing new types of shades and fittings. The amount of light produced was low compared with later bulbs so glass and mirrors were used to reflect the light. Numerous sources were recommended so in addition to the central ceiling light, there would be wall, table and standard lamps. There was a wide range of fittings in traditional forms, as well as some in Art Deco styles in chromium, lacquer and crystal, while the shades could be in etched or patterned glass, silky fabrics or paper. In the finest interiors concealed lighting was all the rage, especially in bathrooms and in some pieces of furniture like dressers.

FIG 5.31: *An advert for gas fires promoting how they were healthier and more comfortable than solid fuel.*

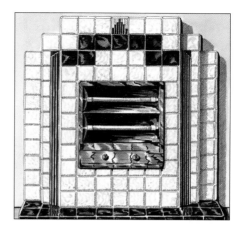

FIG 5.32: *A typical 1930s' fireplace with a modern electric bar heater, an appliance that was usually limited to the most modern houses and apartments.*

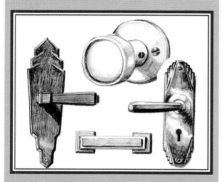

FIG 5.33: *Examples of Art Deco handles. Many were made from Bakelite, a thermosetting plastic named after its inventor, Belgium born chemist Leo H. Baekeland. Its dark brown glossy finish was reinforced with a filler of fibre and wood flour; its resemblance to wood and the way it could be cheaply moulded into fashionable curved shapes made it very popular.*

FIG 5.34: *Part of an advert for Aga cookers. They had been invented in 1922 by Gustaf Dalen, the Swedish Nobel prize-winner, and were licensed for production in Britain in 1929. The Aga was very cheap on fuel and paid itself back over time. It was easier to clean than old ranges, had a cooking tank of 45 litres, also a boiling plate, and a simmering plate with covers to prevent heat loss.*

The most significant change in the home, though, came with the introduction of electrical appliances. From a late Victorian interior with heating and lighting provided by solid fuel and gas, and entertainment limited to the piano, the modern 1930s' household now had an electric iron, a vacuum cleaner, a radio and a gramophone. The main motivation behind many of these devices was that most middle-class homes no longer had a live-in servant. An older member of the family, a daily or a treasure who popped round at certain times to help with the chores of cleaning and cooking was now the usual arrangement for suburban families. In the kitchen the old range cooker, which needed constant attention, was replaced in most homes by a free-standing gas cooker, a much cleaner and easy to control device once Regulo

FIG 5.35: *An advert for gas cookers, which now had thermostatic controls for the oven; this example was available in a blue and white enamelled finish, as well as the colour scheme shown here.*

FIG 5.36: *A gas cooker (left) and free-standing solid fuel hot water boiler (right), a standard combination in most homes.*

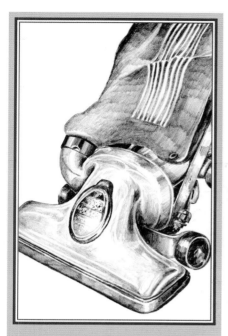

FIG 5.38: *Radios were one of the most distinctive Art Deco features in the house. Some were arched or circular and, as with this example, they were made from Bakelite, which meant that modern shapes could be formed at an affordable price.*

FIG 5.37: *Vacuum cleaners like this Hoover were one of the popular new appliances in the inter-war years.*

controls were introduced after 1923, and some cookers came with a glass door to view the oven – something unheard of before the war. The iron, which had formerly been heated from a hotplate, was now replaced by an electric one that provided a consistent heat. It was easier to use and cleaner, and by the end of the period more than three out of four households with electricity had one. The vacuum cleaner was equally popular, with a variety of upright and cylinder types available from names such as Hoover, Electrolux and Goblin, which are still familiar today, and some even reflected the Art Deco fashion for streamline forms and bold lines in their design.

Perhaps the most distinctive Art Deco piece was the radio and gramophone, or the two combined into a radiogram. As a modern device it was seen appropriate for it to be housed in an up-to-date casing and leading designers came up with innovative streamline and circular types although these were often made from Bakelite, a plastic that simulated wood and added a more acceptable traditional finish but at the same time made them cheaper to produce. Larger gramophones and radiograms were housed in wooden furniture and were free-standing; these again were often in a modern form with Art Deco detailing.

FIG 5.39: *Despite the lady in this advert looking disinterested as she idly twiddles the knobs on this Art Deco wooden-cased radiogram, they were a very popular appliance in the more luxurious home.*

FIG 5.40: *Examples of Art Deco clocks (see also Fig 1.2).*

FIG 5.41: *A rather chilling advert from a British magazine inviting readers to visit Germany in 1937 to see houses built during the 'great nation's stupendous reconstruction' under the Nazis. We will never know how Art Deco could have evolved had it been given a free rein, but with the outbreak of hostilities with Germany two years later those who had been involved with furniture production and interior design devoted themselves to the war effort. Modernist designers made their mark with the Utility furniture that was available for bombed-out families towards the end of the war, paving the way for a more general acceptance of modern furniture and decoration by the mid 1950s, a style more influenced by the space age than the Ancient World.*

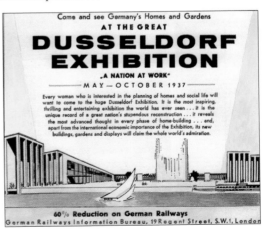

PLACES TO VISIT

D espite the popularity of Art Deco there are surprisingly few places open to the public where you can see the style on display. There is nowhere with an exterior and interior completely built in an Art Deco style and it is perhaps time that the leading building conservation groups started to look at preserving examples of modest Streamline Moderne houses while there are still some intact examples surviving. Below are listed a few places that have 1930s' interiors and the best examples of Art Deco furniture and fittings:

Coleton Fishacre, Brownstone Road, Kingswear, Devon TQ6 0EQ. Telephone: 01803 752466; www.nationaltrust.org.uk

Eltham Palace, Court Yard, Eltham, Greenwich, London SE9 5QE (English Heritage). Telephone: 0208 294 2548 or 0870 333 1181; www.english-heritage.org.uk

Upton House, nr Banbury, OX15 6HT (National Trust). Telephone: 01295 670266; www.nationaltrust.org.uk

There are also a number of places where exceptional houses and buildings in this style can be viewed from the street (please respect owners' privacy when visiting):

Frinton Park Estate, Frinton-on-Sea, Essex CO13 9PG (best examples along Cliff Way, Waltham Way, Quendon Way, and Central Avenue).

Hoover Building, Western Avenue, Greenford, Middlesex UB6 8DW. This is now a Tesco supermarket with the façade retained so it can only be appreciated from the front and side.

Silver End, Witham, Essex CM8 3QQ (main part of estate along Silver Street and at its junction with Boars Tye Road).

The best selection of Art Deco houses, flats and buildings are in London, although they are too scattered and numerous to list here so check these web addresses to find out more details and suggested tours:
www.londoncountrytours.co.uk/londonartdeco.htm
www.vam.ac.uk/vastatic/microsites/1157_art_deco/about/buildings/
www.london-footprints.co.uk/artdecobldgs.htm

GLOSSARY

---••●•---

ARCHITRAVE: The moulding around a door, window or niche.

ASBESTOS: A fire-resistant boarding made from a fibrous silicate mineral used in houses throughout this period. Although safe when intact, it can be very dangerous when broken and the fibres are inhaled.

BAKELITE: A thermosetting plastic with a finish that resembles wood; it can be moulded into any shape.

BALUSTER: Plain or decorated post supporting the stair rail. A balustrade is a row of balusters with a rail along the top.

BARGEBOARD: External vertical boards that protect the ends of the sloping roof on a gable; often decorated.

BAY WINDOW: A window projecting from the façade of a house, of varying height but always resting on the ground.

BITUMEN: A petroleum derivative used for waterproofing flat roofs and forming a damp proof layer in walls or under floors.

BONDING: The way bricks are laid in a wall, with the different patterns formed by alternative arrangements of headers (the short ends) and stretchers (the long side).

CASEMENT WINDOW: A window that is hinged along one side.

CAVITY WALLS: Walls formed from an inner and outer skin of the same or different materials with a thin gap between.

CORNICE: A decorative moulding around the top of an external or internal wall.

DAMP PROOF MEMBRANE (DPM): A waterproof barrier incorporated within walls and ground floors to stop rising damp penetrating the structure above. In this period liquid or sheet bitumen was widely used.

EAVES: The section of the roof timbers under the tiles or slates where they meet the wall, usually protected by a fascia board.

FAÇADE: The main vertical face of the house.

FLUE: The duct for smoke from the fireplace up into the chimney.

GABLE: The pointed upper section of wall at the end of a pitched roof.

HIPPED ROOF: A roof with a slope on all four sides.

INTERNATIONAL STYLE: A contemporary term for houses built under the influence of the Modern movement (named after an American exhibition in 1932).

JAMBS: The sides of an opening for a door or window.

JOISTS: Timber, concrete or steel beams that support the floor.

LINTEL: A horizontal beam that is fitted above a door or window to take the load of the wall above.

LOAD BEARING: A wall that has to support a load, usually floors and a roof.

MODERNISM/MODERNIST: The Modern movement of architecture and architects working in this style. British houses of the 1930s in this style generally had a box-like appearance, with flat roofs and plain white walls, with the priority on their internal arrangement.

MOULDING: A decorative strip of wood, stone or plaster.

PARAPET: The top section of wall as it continues above the roof.

PITCH: The angle by which a roof slopes. A plain sloping roof of two sides is called a pitched roof.

PLASTERBOARD: Sheeting made from a plaster core, with a heavy-duty paper coating, which was used from the 1930s for ceilings and walls.

PLYWOOD: A sandwich of thin layers of wood and adhesive to make a board that is flexible, strong and resistant to warping.

PREFABS: Short for prefabricated houses, referring to those types erected just after the war from surplus materials such as aluminium.

PURLINS: Large timbers that run the length of the roof, supporting the rafters.

RAFTERS: Timbers that are set in a row along the slope of the roof with laths running across their upper surface onto which the tiles are fixed.

RAINWATER TRAP: The metal bucket at the top of a guttering downpipe, which collects water from horizontal lengths.

RENDER: A protective covering for a wall, made from two or three layers of cement.

REVEAL: The sides (jambs) of a recessed window or door opening.

SCREED: A mix of sand and cement used to pour over and form the upper layer of the ground floor. Tiles or carpet were fitted directly to its dried surface.

SCUMBLING: A painted effect for walls, with an opaque coloured glaze applied over a solid colour to give a rough textured or patterned appearance.

SPALLING: The flaking away of pieces of surface material, in this case, concrete.

STREAMLINED: The shaping of cars, planes and trains to make them more aerodynamic, and mirrored on buildings for stylistic reasons.

STRING: The side support panel for a staircase.

STRING COURSE: A horizontal band running across a façade and usually projecting.

STUD WALL: A thin wall made from a timber framework and covered with plasterboard or similar. Used for non load-bearing walls and the front and rear of cross wall houses.

THERMOPLASTIC TILES: A coloured, flat synthetic tile made from a plastic resin, minerals and a pigment.

TRUSS: An arrangement of timber or steel pieces incorporating triangles to form a long beam or support for a roof. When carefully designed, they can stretch further than a single beam.

ULTRA MODERN: A contemporary term for houses built in the Modern style (see also International Style).

VERNACULAR: Buildings made from local materials in styles and method of construction passed down within a distinct area, as opposed to architect-designed structures made from mass-produced materials.

INDEX

A

Aalto, Alvar 12, 57
Art Nouveau 10, 11–12
Arts and Crafts 10, 11, 12,
    15, 19, 24

B

Bakelite 71, 73
bathrooms 43, 63
Bauhaus 14, 15
bedrooms 43, 62–63
Breuer, Marcel 14, 15, 33,
    34, 58

C

carpets and rugs 57, 66–67
Carreras Cigarette Factory,
    Cambden, London 8
Chermayeff, Serge 16
chevrons 20, 21
Chrysler Building, New
    York 13
cinemas (Odeon-style) 15,
    17
Clarke, Arundell 57
Coates, Wells 15, 25, 26–27,
    58

concrete 21–22, 24, 28, 30,
    34, 38, 43, 45, 50
Connell, Amyas 25, 27–29
Constructivism 14, 30
council housing 39–41
Crittall windows 22, 32, 40,
    47, 48
Cubism 13

D

De La Warr Pavilion, Bexhill-
    on-Sea 16, 32
De Stijl 14
Deutsche Werkbund 12
dining rooms 43, 59–60
doors 50–51, 68
Dorn, Marion 57

E

Eltham Palace, London 19

F

fabrics 65–66
fireplaces (and heaters) 54,
    60, 61, 62, 63, 68–71
flats 15, 26, 27, 41–42
floors 23, 66–67

Frinton Park Estate, Frinton,
    Essex 25, 30
furniture 55, 56, 62, 63,
    64–65

G

Gibberd, Frederick 25, 29
glass 22, 48
glass bricks 22–23, 34
Gropius, Walter 13, 14, 15,
    58

H

Heal, Ambrose 15
High and Over, Amersham,
    Bucks 27–28
Hill, Oliver 25, 29–30
Hoffmann, Josef 12
Hollywood Moderne 20,
    21, 45
Hoover Building, West
    London 17

I

International Style (Ultra
    Modern, Horizontal

style) 14, 16, 20, 22, 24, 25, 32, 35, 37, 44
Isokon 15, 27, 58

J

Jazz Moderne 14, 45
Joel, Betty 57, 58

K

kitchens 25–26, 27, 43, 60–62, 72

L

Lawn Road Flats, Hampstead, London 15, 26, 27, 42
Le Corbusier 14, 27, 30
lighting 70
living rooms 43, 59, 60
Lutyens, Sir Edwin 19, 29
Lubetkin, Berthold 30–31

M

Mackintosh, Charles Rennie 12
Mendelsohn, Erich 16
Midland Hotel, Morecombe, Lancs 29
Modern architecture

(Modernism, Modernist) 12–14, 15, 16, 21, 26, 27, 29, 32, 33, 34, 42, 52, 56, 58, 59, 60, 68, 74
Moderne (Streamline Moderne, Suntrap Houses) 16, 20, 21, 22, 24, 36, 37, 42, 43, 44, 45, 53
Morris, William 11
Muthesius, Hermannn 12

P

paint 67
Picasso, Pablo 13
Pritchard, Jack 57, 58

R

radios 11, 57, 60, 63, 72
railings 41, 52
roofs (flat) 7, 16, 20, 22, 24, 44, 45
Ruskin, John 11
Russell, Gordon 15, 27

S

Silver End, Essex 22, 32, 33, 40

sun ray 20, 21, 49
sun roof (sun lounge, sun terrace) 20, 22, 28, 53
Sunspan houses 27

T

Tecton 30, 31
tiles, glass 22–23
tiles (roof) 21, 22, 23, 42
Tutankhamun's tomb 8, 13

V

van de Rohe, Ludwig Mies 13
Vienna Secession 12

W

wallpaper 63, 68
Wierner Werkstatte: 12
windows (metal-framed, sun-trap) 7, 16, 17, 20, 37, 45, 47–49

Y

Yorke, F.R.S. 25

'Hi, I'm Trevor Yorke. I hope you have enjoyed this book. If you have, and want to learn about others I've written, then please go to my publisher's website www.countrysidebooks.co.uk

My titles are available in all platforms – as softcover books and as eBooks.

Follow me on Facebook at trevoryorke-author, and click 'Like' to keep up to date with new titles and offers.

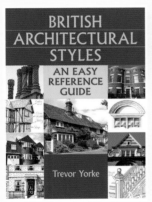
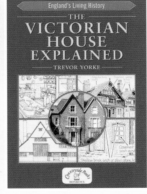
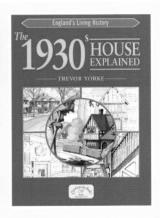

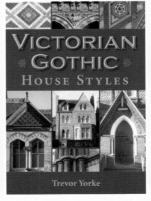